Little People, BIG DREAMS
ALAN TURING

Written by
Maria Isabel Sánchez Vegara

Illustrated by
Ashling Lindsay

Frances Lincoln
Children's Books

Little Alan was a boy from London who went to boarding
school when he was very young. He was shy, and nobody
expected much from him. But often, the quietest people
achieve the most extraordinary things…

At school, Alan spent so much time alone that
he learned to read all by himself. He could also
solve mathematical problems in his head
before his teachers taught him how.

Everything changed when Alan met Christopher. They both shared a passion for math and science and planned to study at Cambridge University together. Alan just couldn't imagine life without his friend…he had fallen in love!

He was ready to move to Cambridge when he got
some terrible news: Christopher had died suddenly.

Alan—who had always been lonely—felt more alone than ever.

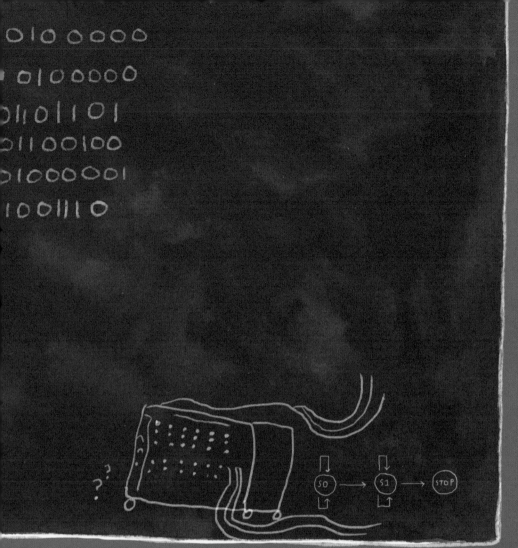

College couldn't cure his broken heart, but it kept his brain busy. Soon, Alan was working on a crazy idea: a machine that could calculate any sum.

Alan's machine was the ancestor of the computers we use today, but he didn't have the chance to build one. Half of Europe had been invaded by Germany, and Alan's destiny was about to change forever.

When Britain joined the war against Germany, Alan and other brilliant minds were hired to break the code used by the Germans to send secret messages to their soldiers.

Mathematicians, chess players, engineers...they all failed to crack Enigma, the code-making machine built by the Nazis. Alan knew that another machine—not a human mind—was the only thing to beat it.

Nobody believed in Alan's idea, so he wrote to the prime minister asking for help to build his device.

Once he got permission, it was just a matter of time before his machine solved the first of many riddles.

Alan's machine helped to win the war and saved millions of lives!

WAR

WAR IS OVER

But his name was kept secret and no one knew he was a hero.
Alan was just happy to go back to work on his computers.

Tragically, Alan became the victim of an unfair law against gay people. He lost his job and was forced to take a bizarre treatment that made him feel very sad.

It took more than 50 years for the British government to apologize for treating Alan—and thousands of gay people—so terribly. They showed great courage by being themselves in a time of great prejudice.

And today, the world is much more open-minded thanks to little Alan, the father of computer science. The boy who believed that those who can imagine anything can create the impossible.

ALAN TURING

(Born 1912 • Died 1954)

1927

c. 1930s

Alan Mathison Turing was born in Paddington, London, as the
second son to a civil servant, Julius, and his wife, Ethel. While his
parents lived and worked overseas in India, Alan and his brother,
John, grew up in houses across England. As a young boy, he was
given a copy of *The Natural Wonders Every Child Should Know*,
which quickly prompted an interest in the scientific world. Educated
at Sherborne School, he met Christopher Morcom—a student in the
year above him with whom Alan fell in love. Christopher's sudden
death at age 19 made Alan more determined than ever to achieve
great things. Alan went on to study mathematics at King's College
in Cambridge and later at Princeton in the US, nurturing an interest

c. 1930s   1950

in probability and logic. He was already working part-time for the British government's Code and Cypher School before World War II broke out. In 1939, Alan began to decipher the military codes used by Germany and its allies at Bletchley Park. He invented a machine that intercepted messages sent by the Germans, which alerted Allied forces to attacks and saved millions of lives. Despite terrible persecution and prejudice for being gay, Alan went on to create the early modern computer in the years after the war. More than half a century later, Britain formally apologized for mistreating Alan and millions of other gay men who suffered in Britain. Today, Alan is considered to be the father of computer science and artificial intelligence.

Want to find out more about **Alan Turing?**

Read this great book:

Code-Breaker and Mathematician Alan Turing (STEM Trailblazer Bios) by Heather E. Schwartz

Brimming with creative inspiration, how-to projects, and useful information to enrich your everyday life, Quarto Knows is a favorite destination for those pursuing their interests and passions. Visit our site and dig deeper with our books into your area of interest: Quarto Creates, Quarto Cooks, Quarto Homes, Quarto Lives, Quarto Drives, Quarto Explores, Quarto Gifts, or Quarto Kids.

Concept and text © 2020 Maria Isabel Sánchez Vegara. Illustrations © 2020 Ashling Lindsay.

First Published in the UK in 2020 by Frances Lincoln Children's Books, an imprint of The Quarto Group.

The Old Brewery, 6 Blundell Street, London N7 9BH, United Kingdom.

T (0)20 7700 6700 F (0)20 7700 8066 **www.QuartoKnows.com**

First Published in Spain in 2019 under the title Pequeño & Grande Alan Turing

by Alba Editorial, s.l.u., Baixada de Sant Miquel, 1, 08002 Barcelona

www.albaeditorial.es

All rights reserved.

Published by arrangement with Alba Editorial, s.l.u. Translation rights arranged by IMC Agència Literària, SL

All rights reserved.

A catalog record for this book is available from the British Library.

ISBN 978-0-7112-4678-2

Set in Futura BT.

Published by Katy Flint • Designed by Karissa Santos

Edited by Rachel Williams • Production by Caragh McAleenan

Manufactured in Guangdong, China CC122019

9 7 5 3 1 2 4 6 8

Photographic acknowledgments (pages 28–29, from left to right) 1. Alan Turing, aged 15, at Westcott House, Sherborne School. © Alan Turing Institute. 2. Alan Turing, c. 1930s © Getty Images 3. Alan Turing, c. 1930s © Rex Shutterstock. 4. Electronic engineer Edward Newman Pilot Model ACE, designed by Alan Turing, 1950 © Jimmy Sime / Stringer / Getty Images.

Collect the
Little People, **BIG DREAMS** series:

FRIDA KAHLO

ISBN: 978-1-84780-783-0

COCO CHANEL

ISBN: 978-1-84780-784-7

MAYA ANGELOU

ISBN: 978-1-84780-889-9

AMELIA EARHART

ISBN: 978-1-84780-888-2

AGATHA CHRISTIE

ISBN: 978-1-84780-960-5

MARIE CURIE

ISBN: 978-1-84780-962-9

ROSA PARKS

ISBN: 978-1-78603-018-4

AUDREY HEPBURN

ISBN: 978-1-78603-053-5

EMMELINE PANKHURST

ISBN: 978-1-78603-020-7

ELLA FITZGERALD

ISBN: 978-1-78603-087-0

ADA LOVELACE

ISBN: 978-1-78603-076-4

JANE AUSTEN

ISBN: 978-1-78603-120-4

GEORGIA O'KEEFFE

ISBN: 978-1-78603-122-8

HARRIET TUBMAN
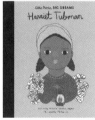
ISBN: 978-1-78603-227-0

ANNE FRANK

ISBN: 978-1-78603-229-4

MOTHER TERESA

ISBN: 978-1-78603-230-0

JOSEPHINE BAKER

ISBN: 978-1-78603-228-7

L. M. MONTGOMERY
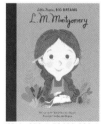
ISBN: 978-1-78603-233-1

JANE GOODALL

ISBN: 978-1-78603-231-7

SIMONe DE BEAUVOIR

ISBN: 978-1-78603-232-4

MUHAMMAD ALI
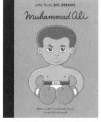
ISBN: 978-1-78603-331-4

STEPHEN HAWKING

ISBN: 978-1-78603-333-8

MARIA MONTESSORI

ISBN: 978-1-78603-755-8

VIVIENNE WESTWOOD

ISBN: 978-1-78603-757-2

MAHATMA GANDHI

ISBN: 978-1-78603-787-9

DAVID BOWIE

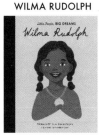

ISBN: 978-1-78603-332-1

WILMA RUDOLPH

ISBN: 978-1-78603-751-0

DOLLY PARTON

ISBN: 978-1-78603-760-2

BRUCE LEE

ISBN: 978-0-7112-4629-4

RUDOLF NUREYEV

ISBN: 978-1-78603-791-6

ZAHA HADID

ISBN: 978-0-7112-4641-6

MARY SHELLEY

ISBN: 978-0-7112-4639-3

MARTIN LUTHER KING JR.

ISBN: 978-0-7112-4567-9

DAVID ATTENBOROUGH

ISBN: 978-0-7112-4564-8

ASTRID LINDGREN

ISBN: 978-0-7112-5217-2

EVONNE GOOLAGONG

ISBN: 978-0-7112-4586-0

BOB DYLAN

ISBN: 978-0-7112-4675-1

ALAN TURING

ISBN: 978-0-7112-4678-2

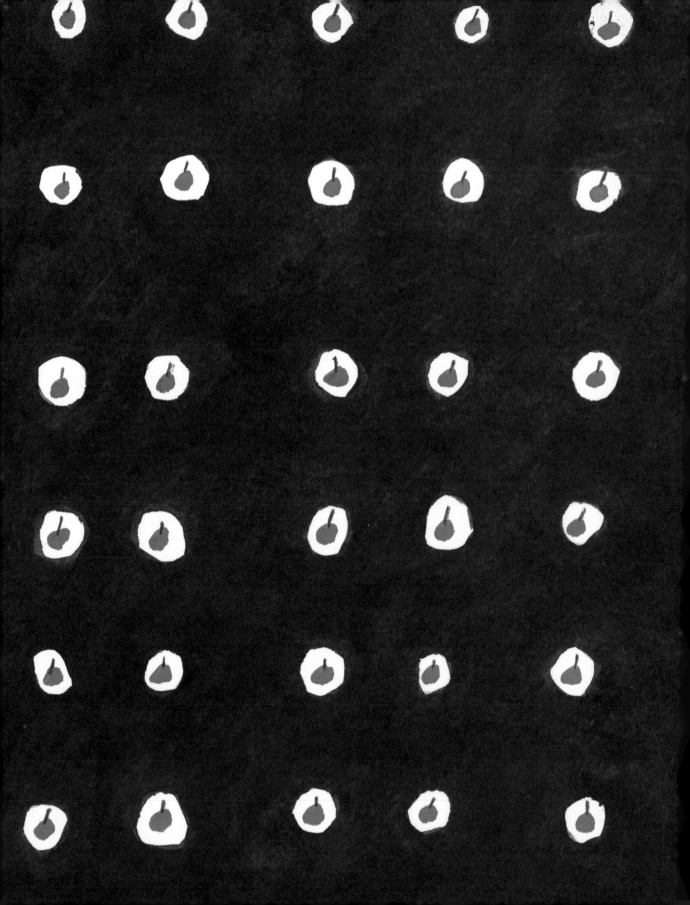